WILDLIFE IN THE NEWS

Scholastic Publications Ltd.,
10 Earlham Street, London WC2H 9RX, UK

Scholastic Inc.,
730 Broadway, New York, NY 10003, USA

Scholastic Tab Publications Ltd.,
123 Newkirk Road, Richmond Hill,
Ontario L4C 3G5, Canada

Ashton Scholastic Pty Ltd.,
PO Box 579, Gosford, New South Wales,
Australia

Ashton Scholastic Ltd.,
165 Marua Road, Panmure, Auckland 6,
New Zealand

First published by Scholastic Publications Ltd, 1990

Created and produced by Ilex Publishers Limited,
29-31 George Street, Oxford OX1 2AJ.

Designed by Designers and Partners, Oxford
and Rogers Jervis, Oxford
Illustrated by Steve Weston

All pictures courtesy of Mark Carwardine/Biotica
except for:
Craven Images/John Craven: p36 bottom; p39 top.
Bruce Coleman Limited: p36 WWF/Timm Rautert top, John Mackinnon
middle right; p37 CB & DW Frith left;
p38 WWF/Kojo Tanaka middle left, John Mackinnon bottom; p39
p41 John Mackinnon top, WWF/ Tim Rautert middle bottom.
Natural History Photographic Agency: p8 F Hanumantha Rao middle
right; p1 and p9 Gerard Laez left; p25 Nigel Dennis bottom right, John
Shaw bottom left.
World Wide Fund for Nature: p38 Halle top, Don Reid middle right;
p40; p41 NF Halbertsma top.
ZEFA: p6 middle; p11 bottom; p21 bottom; p22 middle; p24 middle
right; p25 top; p37 right.
Alain le Garsmeur: p8 top left; p18 top.
Front cover: NHPA/Gerard Laez left; Alain le Garsmeur middle
(with thanks to London Zoo); Tony Stone/Mitch Reardon right.
Back cover: NHPA/Jany Sauvanet left; Tony Stone right.

Printed in Spain by Cayfosa. Barcelona

WILDLIFE SMUGGLING

Wildlife smuggling is big business. Billions of pounds worth of living animals and plants (or their products such as skins, birds' eggs and ivory) are traded all over the world every year. Some of this trade is legal but much of it is not — often because the animals are so rare that there is a danger of their becoming extinct.

Unfortunately, the Spanish beach chimps are only one of the huge number of species, including tortoises, butterflies, cacti, orchids, coral, parrots, hummingbirds, monkeys, even exotic spiders and snakes, that are captured or killed for sale to unscrupulous dealers around the world. The wildlife trade can be very cruel and every year many thousands of animals die slow and painful deaths during the smuggling operations.

Day 5: Still working

Behind this racket are two or three big-time dealers in exotic animals, known to be involved in other kinds of international smuggling. The people concerned are so determined to protect their trade that, on a previous 'undercover' trip to Spain, Mark was chased and threatened by some of the photographers.

The success of the campaign depends very much on the attitudes of people on holiday in Spain. If you visit Spain this year, refuse to have your photograph taken and inform the local police of the photographers' whereabouts. The Spanish authorities have assured us that they will confiscate every animal they can locate.□

ANTI-POACHING PATROL

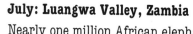

July: Luangwa Valley, Zambia

Nearly one million African elephants have been killed illegally by poachers in the last 10 years; no more than 600,000 are left. Black rhinos are also suffering. In 1970 there were 65,000; today, there may be fewer than 3500.

It seems hard to believe that these two larger-than-life animals could become extinct over much of Africa before the end of the century. But it is true — as we learned on a recent visit to Zambia. ▷

Day 1:
Luangwa Valley

South Luangwa
National Park

Rhino and elephant poaching in Zambia

We were invited to join an anti-poaching patrol organized by the Save the Rhino Trust (SRT) which was set up in 1980 to tackle Zambia's poaching problem. Our patrol worked in the country's most famous national park, the Luangwa Valley, a beautiful woodland area, in the east of the country. The patrol consisted of 10 people: five scouts (each armed with a hunting rifle) and five boys, aged about 15 or 16, who were carrying the food and other equipment and would carry any horns or ivory confiscated by the patrol.

As SRT's Wildlife Warden, Caleb Nkonga, explained to us, these young men are risking their lives to protect Zambia's elephants and rhinos: "We are faced with a colossal and daunting task: to patrol some 10,000 square kilometres of Zambia's wilderness. The terrain is bad and my scouts have a really hard time. They patrol on foot, for an average of 20 days every month, lying in ambush, following trails of destruction left behind by the poachers or using their bush skills to track the gangs down.

"Armed only with hunting rifles – which cannot (by law) be fired except in self-defence – they have to tackle determined and dangerous gangs of professional poachers armed with Kalashnikov AK47s and a range of other sophisticated automatic weapons. They have shoot-outs regularly with poachers – yet there may be only ▷

Day 2:
A close encounter

Black rhinos

TUSK AND HORN

FACTS

Rhino horn, which is made of a hair-like substance, grows from the rhino's skin. Like hair, the horn keeps growing — as much as eight centimetres a year — and, if it is broken off, a new one will grow in its place. The longest-known rhino horn measured more than one and a half metres. Rhinos often use their horns for 'horn-wrestling', when they are arguing with their neighbours over territorial rights; the horns are also used for defence against powerful enemies such as lions and crocodiles.

Elephants' tusks are enlarged teeth, made of a substance known as ivory. They first appear when the animal is about two years old and grow throughout life. There are records of very old bull elephants (more than 60 years old) with tusks as much as three and a half metres long. Elephants use their tusks for feeding — prising bark from trees and digging for roots — and as weapons for fighting.

Fighting

five of them trying to arrest a gang of more than 30. Perhaps not surprisingly, several of my men have been seriously injured."

We spent two days walking through the bush with these brave and dedicated men. We saw a lion, a leopard, several snakes, plenty of hippos and zebras – but only one small herd of elephants – and no rhinos. It was not surprising. In 1975 there were 8000 black rhinos in the Luangwa Valley; today, there are fewer than 200 left in the whole of the country. The elephant population has suffered a similar fate – in the past decade, two in every three of Zambia's elephants have been killed by poachers.

Despite all the problems, SRT *is* making headway. Since operations began, the anti-poaching patrols have made about 1500 arrests, impounded nearly 500 firearms and recovered more than 60 rhino horns and 1300 elephant tusks.

As Caleb told us: "The poachers are finding life more difficult with us around; in many areas, they have been forced to work on a hit-and-run basis and now prefer to remain continually mobile. Nevertheless, the odds are still heavily on the side of the poacher ▷

Day 3:
First night on patrol

ASIAN OR AFRICAN?

The easiest way to tell the difference between an African elephant and an Asian elephant is by their ears. African elephants have enormous ears — much larger than those of their Asian relatives — and they are shaped rather like a map of the African continent.

Their backs also look quite different. The back of an African elephant is gently U-shaped; the back of an Asian elephant is noticeably arched.

Finally, African elephants are slightly taller and heavier animals and both males and females have tusks. In the Asian elephant tusks usually only grow on the males.

and we need to be much more effective in the next few years, or we will be left with nothing to save.''

International efforts to fight the poachers

Most of the horn and ivory ends up outside Africa.

Hunting of the southern white rhino in South Africa is legal, but no trading of its horn is allowed. All rhino horn on the world market is from rhinos killed illegally. More than half the rhino horn goes to the Arabian country of North Yemen to make dagger handles..Other materials (even the horns of much commoner animals) could be used instead, but daggers with rhino-horn handles are prized possessions and much in demand. The remainder is sold mainly in the Far East, where it is ground up and used in hundreds of different medical potions – though many scientists doubt whether any of them really work.

For the few surviving black rhinos the only hope seems to be a controversial programme giving them round-the-clock protection by armed guards. The animals are captured and moved to special fenced ▷

Northern white rhino

enclosures within national parks. Although the rhinos are no longer able to roam free – and the poachers still find ways of getting to them – they are at least a little safer in semi-captivity.

Elephant ivory is carved into ornaments, or made into piano keys, chopsticks, billiard-balls and other goods. The ivory trade has been worth nearly £250 million a year, though recently its value has dropped to nearer £30 million a year. Even so, as many as 100,000 elephants are being killed annually. For a long time a small proportion of ivory sold around the world was from legally killed elephants. Several South African countries (including Zimbabwe, Botswana, Malawi and Mozambique) have long claimed to have ample stocks of elephants and used to cull (shoot) small numbers of them every year to keep their populations under control. The resulting ivory was sold quite legally – but made the illegal ivory trade difficult to stop.

The situation changed dramatically in October 1989, at a crisis meeting to save the elephant from extinction. It was a meeting to discuss an important international agreement called the Convention on International Trade in Endangered Species of Wild Flora and Fauna, or CITES for short. Officials representing the governments of 76 countries voted to ban all international trade in ivory. ▷

Elephant feeding

Afric

Day 4: How many are left?

THE WORLD'S RHINOS

Surprisingly, the black rhino is still one of the most abundant and widespread of the world's five species of rhino. The rarest is the Javan rhino — there are fewer than 70 living in Udjung Kulon National Park, on the island of Java in Indonesia. Next is the Sumatran rhino, with only 750 individuals scattered throughout Sumatra, Malaysia, Thailand and Burma. There are no more than 1700 Indian rhinos, restricted to a few reserves in India and Nepal.

The white rhino is unusual because it exists as two distinct races or sub-species: the northern white and the southern white. The name has nothing to do with its colour — both black and white rhinos are actually grey-brown. There are only 23 surviving northern white rhinos, all living in the Garamba National Park, in Zaire; but there are just under 5000 southern white rhinos, living in southern Africa.

The ban came into force on 18 January 1990. But member countries are allowed to 'take a reservation' on any CITES ban they do not like. Almost immediately Zimbabwe took such a reservation on the ivory ban, which means that the ivory trade there can continue quite legally. Several other countries are considering similar reservations – so the ban is unlikely to be as successful as the conservationists had originally hoped. It is also a sad fact that, while there is money to be made, the poaching is likely to continue – as experience with rhinos has already shown.

Time is running out

A great deal is being done already to save Africa's elephants and rhinos – but more efforts are needed to fight the poachers. Stricter penalties are required and tighter controls at the business end of the poaching operations. The police and Special Investigations Teams in Zambia and other countries, who tackle the poachers in the field, need more financial support and larger squads of skilled wardens.

Most important of all is the need to change people's attitudes towards ivory and rhino horn. If no-one was willing to buy the trophies, they would drop in value and the poachers would be forced to stop their illegal activities.

But time is rapidly running out. ☐

Day 5:
In Luangwa Valley

A black rhino at a waterhole

Southern white rhino

THE JUNGLE BUNGLE

Day 1:
A little girl approaches us...

April: Perinet, Madagascar

The train journey from Antananarivo, the capital of Madagascar, to the small town of Perinet, near the east coast of the country, took about four hours. We travelled past paddy fields and villages, through forests and tunnels, over small bridges, and along the edges of cliffs and cascading rivers.

As we unloaded our gear from the train, a little girl approached us holding a bunch of flowers in her hand. We gave her a few coins and she smiled happily before running off down the platform. We had a quick lunch at the Hotel Buffet de la Gare (which is the only place to stay in Perinet) and set off for the rain forest reserve nearby.

Searching for the indri

We were visiting the Perinet Special Reserve to search for a wonderful lemur known as the indri, which is now in acute danger of extinction because of the widespread destruction of its rain forest home.

The largest member of the lemur family, the indri is almost a metre tall. It has virtually no tail, a teddy-bear face and striking black-and-white markings on its body. An expert at leaping from tree to tree, it uses its long back legs like a spring. ▷

A NEW LEMUR

DISCOVERED

In 1986 an exciting discovery was made in Madagascar. A new species of lemur was found in a small area of rain forest near the town of Ranomafana, in the south-east of the country. It has been named the golden bamboo lemur.

The new species looks rather like a monkey, to which it is distantly related. Roughly a metre in length, half of which consists of a black-tipped tail, it has small round ears, golden eyebrows, orange cheeks and a rich reddish-brown coat. Two individuals of the new species, a male and a female, have been captured by scientists in Madagascar. They are now in captivity in the zoo at Antananarivo, the capital city, where they are being studied closely.

There are two other species of bamboo lemur living in the Ranomafana area: the grey gentle lemur, which is quite common in Madagascar, and the greater bamboo lemur, which is so

Indris tend to live high up in the forest canopy and spend most of the night fast asleep or quietly dozing. They spend all day feeding, though the best times to see them are either early in the morning or shortly before dusk, when they are more active.

It was late in the afternoon when we first entered the forest. Within an hour, we had heard the indris' melodious calls echoing through the trees. It was the rather eerie sound of two troops calling to each other across the forest. We followed their calls for several kilometres before we saw a sudden movement high above the ground, as one of the animals leapt into a nearby tree. It propelled itself backwards, travelling nearly 10 metres through the air while turning around in time to land, face forward, on the next tree.

As we looked up a second indri followed in hot pursuit, leaping across the gap between the two trees with the skill of an acrobat. The indri troop seemed almost as interested in us as we were in them, and looked back down at us with wide, staring eyes. We watched one another until it was almost dark. Then we left them to make our way back to the hotel at the railway station. ▷

Jungle wildlife is threatened

Day 2:
Madagascar's rain forest

rare that it was believed to be extinct until its rediscovery in 1972.

In recent years, large areas of the forest have been chopped down by loggers, and by local farmers for land crops, so the lemurs and all the other animals living there are at risk.

However, the discovery of the golden bamboo lemur may have saved the day. It has encouraged the Government of Madagascar to consider establishing the forest as a national park. With immediate intervention of this kind, Ranomafana and all its wildlife could still be saved.

As scientists explore new areas of rain forest in Madagascar, more lemur species are likely to be identified. The latest discovery is the golden-crowned sifaka, which has a shock of golden orange on the crown of its head. There are only a few hundred of these beautiful animals left, making them one of the most endangered of all the lemurs.

Day 3:
Pet snake

Gecko

A surprise at the railway station

We arrived to find the station platform full of children, all giggling and jostling for position to get a good look at us. They had heard that we were interested in wildlife and had brought a bizarre collection of animals to show us. The station suddenly became a treasure house of unique creatures that we had not seen anywhere else in the world.

There was a five-centimetre-long spider; a cockroach that hissed when it was angry; and even a tiny scorpion, running around in the bottom of a shoe box. One little boy had brought us a chameleon which was almost 30 centimetres long. Madagascar is home to about half the world's chameleons – 40 species in all. ▷

Another boy had with him an appealing creature that looked rather like a small hedgehog with an extraordinary long nose; it was a tenrec, another animal unique to Madagascar.

Finally, there was a man from the village with a writhing and wriggling sack. Smiling, he put his hand inside and pulled out a beautiful snake, a kind of boa, about a metre in length. Snakes, he told us, are very common in Madagascar. Apparently, not one of them is dangerous to people.

Disappearing rain forests

Madagascar has been in the news a great deal recently. Many of the animals and plants we saw there are threatened with extinction because their beautiful forest homes are being chopped and burned down.

The same is true in many other countries in the tropics. At least 15 million hectares of rain forest, or 'jungle' as we sometimes call it, is being chopped down, cleared by bulldozers and burned every year. That is an area more than three times the size of Switzerland.

If this continues, all the world's jungles will be gone within 40 years. This destruction has been headlined 'The Jungle Bungle' and could become the greatest disaster the natural world has known since the disappearance of the dinosaurs 65 million years ago. ▷

TREATING CANCER

WITH FLOWERS

For centuries a pretty little flower from Madagascar, called the rosy periwinkle, has been used by tribal witchdoctors as a medicine. When modern scientists investigated the flower for themselves it was found to contain a number of important medicinal substances.

Now the rosy periwinkle is used in drugs that fight childhood leukaemia, Hodgkin's disease and several other cancers. It has been incredibly successful. In 1960, four children out of every five with leukaemia died; now four out of every five survive.

Rosy Periwinkle

Many people believe that a very close relative of the rosy periwinkle, known in the scientific world as *Catharanthus coriaceus*, may be even more valuable in the battle against cancer. But it is an endangered species and only a very small population is known to survive in the wild; if it is allowed to become extinct we shall never know how useful it might have been.

The United States National Cancer Institute thinks that more than 2000 types of rain forest plants could be used in the world-wide campaign to beat cancer.

Day 4:
Cleared rain forest

The
Amazon Jungle

Why are the forests disappearing?

Tribal people have been living in jungles for about 40,000 years. They have always chopped down trees for firewood and building materials, but they have taken great care to harvest the forests carefully to avoid losing them altogether. These days, however, people from the cities and other parts of the world are infiltrating the forests. Their main interest is just one product – wood. Tropical hardwood is very valuable.

In earlier days, it used to take a team of workers a whole day to chop down a giant tree. Now, with mechanical saws, it takes one person about 10 minutes. But it is not just the timber trade that is destroying the forests. So, too, are the cattle barons. Enormous areas of forest in Central and South America have been cleared to make room for cattle. Nearly all the beef produced on these ranches goes to the United States and ends up in 'junk' food. As one expert put it, "They are turning forests into hamburgers!"

It is also the poor people who live in and around the forests who are doing the damage. Hundreds of millions of peasant families have no choice but to eke out a meagre living on the poor forest soils. They fell trees to make a clearing, and then plant seeds. But after two or three harvests nothing more will grow. So the peasants move on, ▽

deeper into the jungle, and do the same thing again. What else can they do? They have to survive and there is nowhere else to go.

Does it matter if the rain forests disappear?

It is not only the rich jungle wildlife that is in peril – if the rain forests disappear, we will all be affected. Every time we eat some chocolate, stick a postage stamp to an envelope, chew gum, wash our hair, play golf or sit on a wickerwork chair we are using a rain forest product.

The rain forest trees help to conserve soil, by binding it to the hillsides; and they regulate our supply of water by holding it like a sponge and releasing it slowly and steadily. They can even influence the world's climate, by absorbing the heat of the sun and by controlling the level of carbon dioxide gas in the atmosphere. ▷

Day 5:
Mark in the Jungle

How can we stop the Jungle Bungle?

There are still large areas of jungle left – covering an area roughly equal in size to the United States of America. Already, a great deal is being done to protect the jungle: there are over 600 different rain forest parks and reserves around the world.

But these protected areas cover less than five per cent of the remaining forest and, even then, some of the parks and reserves are still being destroyed. The real hope for saving them lies in careful management, so that the rain forests can provide a satisfactory livelihood for local people – and earn governments money – while being protected at the same time.

Time is running out fast. But saving the rain forests is one of the most urgent conservation problems facing the world today. □

Jungle tree

JUNGLE FACTFILE

- A typical patch of rain forest, just 10 kilometres square, contains as many as 1500 species of flowering plants, up to 750 different trees, 400 species of bird, 100 species of reptile, 60 different amphibians, 150 kinds of butterfly and many thousands — possibly hundreds of thousands — of other insects.

- Some of the world's most seriously endangered animals live in jungles, including orang-utans, gorillas, jaguars, Sumatran rhinos, imperial parrots and birdwing butterflies.

- Jungles are also the home of tribal peoples, who are struggling for survival along with the wildlife. Brazil had nearly nine million Indians in the year 1500; it has fewer than 200,000 today.

- The largest flower in the world is found in the jungles of south-east Asia. Called the rafflesia, it can measure nearly a metre across but, despite its impressive appearance, has a horrible smell rather like rotting meat.

- The biggest and most famous of all the world's rain forests is the Amazon, with its great river that is fed by more than 10,000 tributaries. The river is so huge that one-fifth of all the fresh water on Earth flows through it every day. The river bursts into the Atlantic Ocean with such force that 150 kilometres out to sea you can still taste fresh water.

THE PLIGHT OF THE WHALES

Mark whale-watching

Day 1:
Hvalfjordur (whaling station)

June: Iceland

About 100 kilometres north of Reykjavik, the capital city of Iceland, lies Hvalfjordur whaling station. Situated on Iceland's spectacular south-western coast, it is – thankfully – one of the last active whaling stations in the world.

We travelled to Iceland early one June to witness the arrival of the first whales of the season, which usually lasts until nearly the end of September. As we watched, a single ship arrived at the station with two enormous fin whales tied to its sides, each almost as long as the ship itself. It was one of the most saddening sights either of us had seen in a long time.

Whales are disappearing

The two whales had been inflated with air and were being brought back to Hvalfjordur for processing. There to greet them were massive flocks of gulls and fulmars, which feed on the bloody remains. But we were more horrified to see dozens of tourists watching from the shoreline – and to learn that the whaling station had become a major tourist attraction. How can the sight of a slaughtered whale be thought of as 'entertainment'?

A few centuries ago, anyone visiting Iceland would have seen enormous numbers of whales, of many species, around the coast. Today the whales are still there – but their numbers have decreased so much that you have to be very lucky to see one. One American ▷

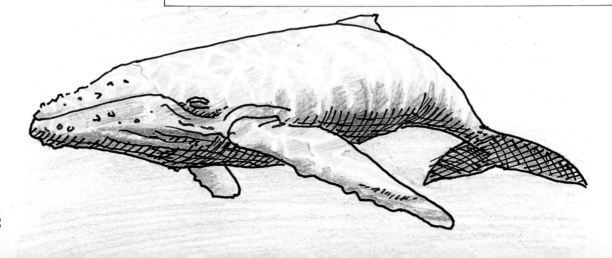

tourist, on a day trip to Hvalfjordur, summed it up when she explained to us that a visit to the whaling station was the only way she could be sure of seeing a whale in Iceland.

Around the world more than one and a half million whales have been killed already this century — by many different countries — and several whale species are now on the verge of extinction.

Modern technology against the whales

Until quite recently, tiny boats were used by the whalers, to attack whales entering the calmer waters of the Icelandic fjords. Nowadays the whalers have ships which can easily catch up with the fleeing animals, with lots of technical equipment on board including explosive harpoons which are fired from cannons.

In some countries, whaling operations are even more efficient and sophisticated than in Iceland. The ships have special tracking equipment, from which the animals cannot hide. It means that the whalers don't need to see the whales until a second before they fire the harpoon. Also special 'factory ships' sailing with the whaling vessels enable the animals to be processed far out at sea.

All in the name of science

Iceland is not alone in continuing to kill whales. Japan and Norway are also continuing the hunt — even though the damage which has already been done is there for all to see. Between them, the three nations kill nearly 400 fin, sei and minke whales each year. ▷

whale meat

AN INTERNATIONAL
P R O B L E M

The root cause of the whaling tragedy is that the whales' kingdom is the ocean — which belongs to everyone and no-one — so there can be no laws to protect them. There is, however, an international agreement called 'The Whaling Convention' which has been signed by the governments of more than 40 countries.

A major breakthrough came in 1985 when representatives of these countries decided to ban all commercial whaling. Most countries welcomed the decision, others, including the Soviet Union, have agreed to the ban in the years since.

But whaling nations cannot be made to agree to the ban. As a result it is very difficult for other countries — or conservation organizations — to force the whalers to stop.

Many people have tried. Greenpeace members, for example, have driven inflatable boats inbetween whales and the harpoon guns in a desperate bid to save some of these mighty animals and to bring the horror of whaling to the attention of the world.

But still the whalers continue hunting in defiance of this world 'peace treaty' with the whales.

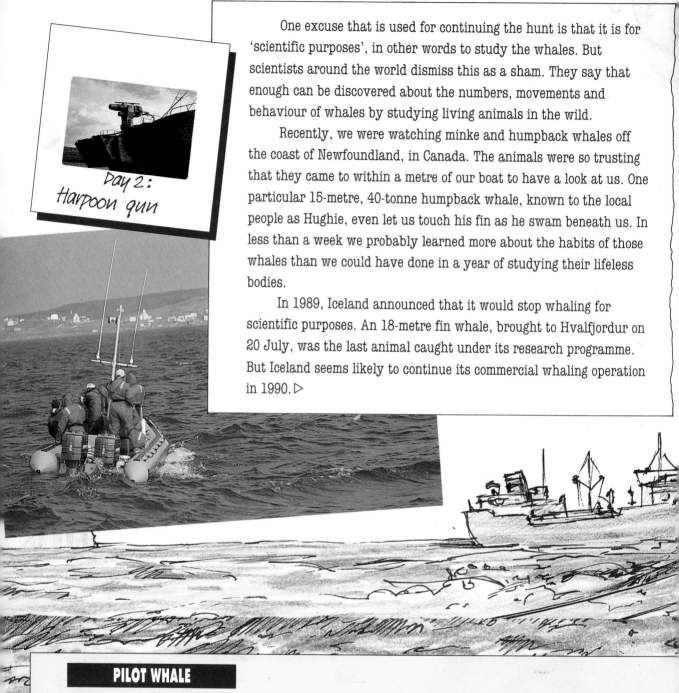

Day 2:
Harpoon gun

One excuse that is used for continuing the hunt is that it is for 'scientific purposes', in other words to study the whales. But scientists around the world dismiss this as a sham. They say that enough can be discovered about the numbers, movements and behaviour of whales by studying living animals in the wild.

Recently, we were watching minke and humpback whales off the coast of Newfoundland, in Canada. The animals were so trusting that they came to within a metre of our boat to have a look at us. One particular 15-metre, 40-tonne humpback whale, known to the local people as Hughie, even let us touch his fin as he swam beneath us. In less than a week we probably learned more about the habits of those whales than we could have done in a year of studying their lifeless bodies.

In 1989, Iceland announced that it would stop whaling for scientific purposes. An 18-metre fin whale, brought to Hvalfjordur on 20 July, was the last animal caught under its research programme. But Iceland seems likely to continue its commercial whaling operation in 1990. ▷

PILOT WHALE

HUNT

Halfway between Scotland and Iceland is a group of small, craggy, mist-shrouded islands called the Faroes. On a few horrific days each year the islands make news headlines around the world as the Faroese people, in motor-powered fishing boats, drive longfin pilot whales into shallow waters to kill them.

The frightened animals are held by a 'gaff' (a kind of hook) and then stabbed with knives. As the world looks on in horror, the sea turns red with blood and the whales die slow and painful deaths.

For centuries, the Faroese have been killing the friendly, six-metre long, jet black pilot whales for food. More than 230,000 of them have been killed in the past 250 years; and there is also evidence of the hunters killing dolphins, porpoises and killer whales. Whale meat was once an important source of food for

A bleak future for the world's whales?

At one time, it is true that whales were very important to the whaling nations. In hard times, their meat provided a life-saving source of food and, in the days before gas and electricity, their oil and blubber were burned to make light. Over the years whale products have been used in thousands of ways, from perfume and candlewax to margarine and drum skins. But these days everything that is obtained from a whale can be manufactured artificially. So the whaling nations are being really stubborn – because hunting whales is no longer necessary.

The whales have already paid a dreadful price for being useful to humans. There is no need to kill them any more. □

Whale!

Humpback whale breaching

Faroe Islands

the 46,000 islanders. But nowadays they have a high standard of living and import all the food they need. They eat only one meal of whale meat a week — so it is hardly an essential source of nourishment any more.

One of the worst aspects — or so it seems to people watching the hunt — is how much the Faroese seem to enjoy the killing. It looks almost like a traditional festival or a national sport.

For many years, leading international conservation groups have been trying to persuade the Faroese to stop. They are concerned about the cruelty involved — and about the future of the pilot whale populations. But the response from the islands has been disappointing. The Government continues to claim that whale meat is still needed, and that the hunt is a national tradition which it sees no reason to stop.

THE GIANT PANDAS OF WOLONG

May: Wolong, China

It is 40 bumpy kilometres up a rough road through the mountains before you reach the Wolong Panda Research Centre, on the banks of the cascading Pitiao River. Low-level functional buildings are dwarfed on either side by the sheer slopes of a narrow valley that is densely wooded and always coated in wispy mist.

Nothing advertises what happens here. No sign-posts, no hoardings, no little shops selling souvenirs. Just a small but vital symbol of a giant panda on one of the walls. Tourists are not allowed even to start along the winding road to Wolong. The home of the panda is a 'forbidden area', and the small team working on BBC TV's *Newsround China* was the first Western film crew to be granted the right to visit the centre and the surrounding reserve. ▷

Daxiongmao = panda

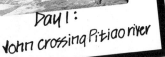

Day 1:
John crossing Pitiao river

Wolong Natural Reserve

Wolong Natural Reserve, in Sichuan Province, is the largest of the 12 panda reserves in China. It is a mountainous area of 2000 square kilometres with an outstanding variety of wildlife, including about 100 species of mammals, 230 different birds and 20 species of reptiles.

Wolong's declining panda population

Until quite recently, there were between 130 and 150 giant pandas roaming within its borders. But in the past few years many of these animals have literally starved to death because of a sudden, and very serious, shortage of bamboo. Nowadays only a quarter of the land at Wolong is suitable for pandas, so if the bamboo dies out there is nowhere left for them to go. ▷

THE GIANT PANDA:

WHAT IS IT?

Until 1869, no Western scientist had ever seen a giant panda. Then the French missionary Père Armand David was shown a panda skin during a visit to Sichuan, in China. He assumed that it belonged to the bear family — one of its local names is, indeed, 'white bear'.

Sharing a meal

Eating bamboo

But many scientists have their doubts about the accuracy of Père David's assumption. Some still believe that it is a bear. However, many experts place it in the raccoon family, because of its raccoon-like bones and teeth. Others claim it is so unusual that it should be placed in an entirely new group of animals, with its close relative the red panda.

The Chinese name for the giant panda is 'daxiongmao', which means great bear-cat. But while no one is certain whether it is a bear or a raccoon — it is certainly not a cat!

Day 2:
Wolong Panda Research Centre

Giant Panda

Two hours' trek up the hills from the Wolong Centre is a field station. Researchers there told us that out of the 18 pandas in the area they monitor, at least eight had died. Three of them were considered to be 'part of the team'. They had been wearing radio tracking collars, fitted by the scientists to help them monitor the animals' movements.

Other pandas are luckier. They are spotted in time by search teams, or by local peasants who claim rewards for information about sick animals. Rescuers have found some alive but too weak to move, with their heads resting on their front paws, waiting for death.

The research centre has several large pens – and a well-equipped hospital – for rescued pandas. It also has what local workers touchingly call 'the sports field' – a stoutly-walled area where the pandas are sometimes taken for exercise. ▽

Because of the current shortage of bamboo, the captives' diet is being boosted with rye grass, originally from New Zealand. It is an important breakthrough, because if rye grass could be grown alongside bamboo in the mountains, the food crisis could be solved. So far, the pandas certainly seem to like it.

Detective work to count pandas

Important research is being done by the team at Wolong, led by Chinese scientists and experts from the World Wide Fund for Nature. In particular, the team has studied the pandas' dependence on bamboo, and is carrying out a survey to establish just how many animals still survive in the reserve. Pandas are difficult creatures to observe in the wild, largely because the bamboo forests in which they live are usually so dense that a panda is invisible at a distance of only five metres. Like detectives, the researchers have to look for clues of the pandas' presence – such as droppings or signs of feeding activity. ▷

Day 3:
Wolong's Misty hills

Moving people out of the panda reserve

In recent months, attempts have also been made to persuade the people of the Chang tribe, who live in Wolong, to move farther down the valley where a new village, called Genda, is being built for them. They are sturdy people who have lived in this bleak, cold valley for many centuries, and now suddenly they have been asked to move – for the sake of the pandas! Modern houses have been allocated to them, with electricity and tap water, and land to grow their crops. But the move is voluntary and the families have so far refused to leave the upper valley of Wolong, so the authorities are now considering providing them with a special area within the reserve. Elsewhere, the fields can be turned back to bamboo – and the pandas will have a better chance of survival.

New village at Genda

Breeding pandas at Wolong

In the meantime, the research centre hopes to breed pandas from their healthy captives. There were great celebrations on 10 August ▷

Panda in captivity

PANDAS IN ZOOS

The first live panda to be seen in the West was a cub called 'Su-Lin'. She was smuggled out of China, in 1937, by an American lady who sold her to Chicago's Brookfield Zoo. Since then China has given about 30 pandas to zoos around the world, as expressions of friendship. Sixteen of these are still alive today. In addition, China itself has about 70 pandas in captivity. So there are fewer than 100 pandas in zoos and research stations world-wide.

Since 1963 about 50 baby pandas have been born in various zoos and research stations around the world. About half of them are still alive today. But despite a great deal of work on captive pandas in zoos, there has been surprisingly little success in efforts to breed them.

The main problem is that, because giant pandas are so rare, most nations or zoos have only one pair or a single animal. Male and female pandas do not always like one another — the females, in particular, are choosy about their mates. Therefore it is difficult to pair them successfully.

Even if they mate and the female gives birth, the chances of the young panda cubs surviving are low, as they probably are in the wild. A baby panda weighs only about 100 grammes at birth, so it needs careful looking after.

A breeding captive population is a vitally important back-up to the panda conservation programme. 1988 was London Zoo's fiftieth year of keeping giant pandas and it sent its only panda, a male called Chia-Chia, to Mexico City to pair with a seven-year-old female called Tohui. Everyone is extremely hopeful that a successful mating will take place and that this will encourage a more regular mixing of the world's captive pandas.

Beijing Zoo.

1986, when the first baby was born. Among the earliest visitors to meet the Very Important Baby was HRH Prince Philip, the President of the World Wide Fund for Nature. The Prince named the new baby panda Lan-Tian, or Blue Sky. New-born pandas are so tiny that they are terribly vulnerable to infection, changes in the weather and malnutrition – so baby Lan-Tian's survival was a great triumph.

Lan-Tian's mother is Li-Li, who is thought to be about 18 years old and weighs a little over 100 kilograms. Li-Li (the Chinese nearly always repeat the name as a sign of affection) was rescued from the ▷

Prince Philip + Lan-tian

THE PLIGHT OF

THE PANDA

Last year, the World Wide Fund for Nature issued a statement, warning that the giant panda would become extinct in the wild by the end of this century unless drastic steps were taken.

Pandas are among the rarest creatures on earth, living only within a restricted range in the mountains of south-western China. There may be fewer than 1000 survivors left, though some estimates suggest that their population has already dropped as low as 400.

One of the reasons is poaching. Sometimes this is accidental: local villagers set snares to catch musk deer and the pandas get caught and killed in them. However, the pandas themselves have long been hunted for their skins and the poaching continues, even though the giant panda is protected by law and anyone caught trapping one, either for its pelt or for food, is sent to prison. Pandas are so rare and beautiful that, sadly, their skins will always be in demand by wealthy collectors.

In April 1988, China's Minister of Forestry revealed that 146 panda skins had been discovered in Sichuan Province. That is more than fifteen per cent of the total world panda population.

Habitat destruction and a lack of suitable food are even more important threats to the panda's survival. In recent years about 150 of the animals have starved to death.

wild in the late 1970s, when she was facing starvation, and has lived in Wolong ever since. The father is Quan-Quan, who is only eight years old and weighs about 90 kilograms. He was found unconscious in the wild with a head injury, after falling from a cliff, and was taken to Chengdu Zoo. After treatment and rest, he was taken to Wolong and introduced to Li-Li.

The mating of Li-Li happened completely naturally – the scientists were not called in to help, as they have done at so many zoos around the world. In fact, Quan-Quan was only the second captive male in China to mate successfully. Being behind bars seems to put them off – and the fact that the females are only on heat for two or three days a year does not make things any easier!

Other hopes lie with Jia-Jia and Ping-Ping – both females – and Shan-Shan and Ling-Gang – both males. All are mature and healthy. Since our visit, they have been joined by at least five other pandas, all rescued from starvation in the nearby mountains. Although now captive, at least they are still within sight and smell of their beloved, misty mountains.

The scientists at Wolong had hoped that baby Lan-Tian was the beginning of what would become a highly-successful breeding programme. But sadly, in the spring of 1989, she died. Instead of being a hopeful symbol for the future, she has become another loss in the long, sad struggle for the survival of her species. □

Li-Li and baby Lan-Tian

Panda cub

The problem is that only two types of bamboo, the fountain and umbrella varieties, are hardy enough to grow on both the humid ravine floors and the cold mountain slopes, where giant pandas live. Both kinds follow a 50-year cycle, so that roughly twice in every century they bloom, drop their seeds and then die. It takes another six years for them to regenerate and, in the meantime, there is nothing for the pandas to eat.

In ancient times, when bamboo died in one area, the pandas were able to move somewhere else to find their food. But in recent years farmers have been taking more and more land for agriculture and gradually pushing the pandas higher up the mountain slopes. So nowadays the animals have nowhere else to go, and eventually starve.

Chinese scientists, the World Wide Fund for Nature and other conservationists around the world are now deeply concerned about the panda's future and every effort is being made to save it from extinction.

Broken bamboo

THE BATTLE FOR THE BEACHES

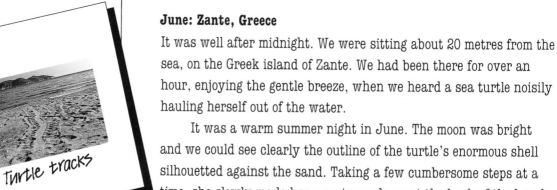

turtle tracks

June: Zante, Greece

It was well after midnight. We were sitting about 20 metres from the sea, on the Greek island of Zante. We had been there for over an hour, enjoying the gentle breeze, when we heard a sea turtle noisily hauling herself out of the water.

It was a warm summer night in June. The moon was bright and we could see clearly the outline of the turtle's enormous shell silhouetted against the sand. Taking a few cumbersome steps at a time, she slowly made her way towards us at the back of the beach. It took a full 20 minutes for her to reach a point about three metres from where we were watching. After a brief rest, though still puffing and panting, she began to dig a large hole.

We hardly dared to breathe, in case we frightened her. But she was so intent on kicking the sand away with her back flippers that she probably did not even know we were there. After a few minutes ▷

Day 1:
Turtle Bay, Zante

we decided to risk shining a torch to see what was happening. The giant turtle, a full metre in length, hardly seemed to notice.

When the hole was finished, it consisted of a large scrape, about a metre in diameter. In the centre was a cylindrical chamber, some 30 centimetres deep. As we watched, the turtle began to lay her eggs in the deepest part of the nest. By the time she had finished we had counted 83 altogether. Very carefully we picked out one of the eggs to take a closer look: it was round, white and soft to touch, about the size of a table tennis ball. Having quietly replaced it, we watched in awe as the turtle painstakingly covered all her eggs with sand.

Once she had made the laborious trek back to the sea, we checked our watches. The whole process had taken nearly two hours.

A place in the sun for both turtles and tourists?

Every summer sea turtles, such as the loggerhead turtle we saw, migrate in their thousands across the world's oceans to lay their eggs on soft, sandy beaches. However, in recent years their populations have been declining almost everywhere. One of the reasons is that many of the beaches, which the turtles have had to themselves for centuries, are now full of people. We were in Greece to find out whether there is a place in the sun for both turtles and tourists.

Zante is a beautiful place, with rolling hills crested with cypresses and olive groves and large vineyards in the valleys. The golden beaches in the south of the island are the nesting grounds for one of the few remaining populations of loggerhead turtles anywhere in Europe.

Fifteen years ago, tourists were virtually unknown in the Zante turtles' territory. However, the island now has its own international airport and there are holiday-makers everywhere. People drive their▷

THREATENED

SEA TURTLES

The loggerhead turtle is one of seven different kinds of sea turtle, the others being the green, hawksbill, Atlantic ridley, Pacific ridley, leatherback and flatback. The largest is the leatherback, which is an incredible animal that grows to nearly two metres long. With the sole exception of the flatback, they are all threatened species.

One of the major difficulties in sea turtle conservation is that the animals take no notice of national boundaries. They swim freely from one country to another. Therefore because different countries have different laws and attitudes towards them, the turtles can be protected in some parts of their range but not in others.

Sea turtle experts from

turtle 'souvenirs'

around the world have drawn up an international Sea Turtle Conservation Strategy. One of the aims of the strategy is to build up sea turtle numbers to their former abundance. Nature reserves and marine national parks are being established, there are round-the-clock protection schemes, and many countries are now working to stop international trade in the animals.

cars on to many of the beaches and the latest hit records blast out of beach-side cafés. This is bad news for the turtles. They do not like noise, they are disoriented by bright lights (which cause them to crawl inland instead of towards the sea) and they hate crowds. Water-skiing and other sea sports involving speed-boats add to the many hazards the turtles now have to face.

Sensibly, the females usually wait until the relative safety of darkness before coming ashore. Even then, they often come face-to-face with dozens of eager tourists, each armed with a torch and a camera. If they persevere and lay their eggs there is every chance that, next morning, sunbathers will unwittingly stamp and tread on them. If the eggs survive the young hatchlings, no more than a few centimetres long, will emerge some seven or eight weeks later. Most of them quickly fall prey to fish, birds and other predators. Some will be picked up and disturbed by tourists. Only a few will survive. ▷

Day 2:
Turtle protection sign

TURTLE CONSERVATION

IN PAKISTAN

Recently we visited Karachi, in Pakistan, where there is a very impressive conservation programme to protect the green and Pacific ridley turtles which nest along the sandy beaches near the city. Known as Hawkes Bay and Sandspit, the two beaches are considered to be among the top 11 sites for nesting sea turtles anywhere in the world.

Both turtles have been protected in the area since 1972. However, they are still in demand in Pakistan: their shells are turned into ornaments such as ashtrays, their meat is used to make turtle soup and their eggs are considered, by some people, to be a tasty delicacy. Therefore, in 1980, this ambitious project was set up.

Every night, the most important stretch of beach is patrolled by special turtle guards. Whenever they find a female digging a nest they wait patiently nearby and, as soon as she has finished laying, gather up her eggs. These are then taken to turtle enclosures, which are guarded 24 hours a day. Inside the enclosures are artificial 'nests', in which the eggs are placed.

When the tiny turtle hatchlings emerge from their new homes, several weeks later, they are carefully placed

Efforts to keep turtles and tourists apart

Some of the turtles' favourite beaches have been partially protected by law since 1980. There was even a new Presidential decree, signed on 14 December 1986, which provided complete protection for them in a large bay and along an important nesting beach.

However, many hotel owners and other people on Zante want to encourage unrestricted growth in tourism and they completely ignore all the turtle protection laws. Their vans and bulldozers, used to clear seaweed from the beaches, destroy many turtle nests. They have built walls, small hotels, restaurants and houses on or close to the nesting grounds. Some hotel owners have smashed the turtle protection signs and have even threatened deliberately to prevent the turtles from nesting, by killing the adults and digging up their nests.

This is all highly illegal – but the islanders are getting away with it because the turtle protection laws are not being enforced. The Greek Prime Minister, the new Chief of Police on Zante and the Greek press, television and radio are all on the side of the sea turtles. However, unless the laws are strictly enforced, it seems almost inevitable that there will soon be nowhere left for the animals to go.

In the meantime, the situation continues to worsen: there are more tourists and fewer turtles on Zante now than ever before.□

Hawkes Bay turtle enclosure

Green turtle hatchlings

in a bucket and carried down to the sea to be released. In one six-year period, no fewer than 185,453 green turtle hatchlings and 11,407 Pacific ridley hatchlings were released in this way. A further 36,279 hatchlings were collected on the beach and carried to the sea by hand.

One of the most important aspects of Pakistan's turtle conservation project is to educate people about the existence and value of sea turtles. Guided tours are arranged for visitors to the beaches and many parties of school children have been taken for exciting night-time vigils to watch the animals.

The project has been immensely successful: the turtles and their eggs are now well protected, and even the local people have begun to take an interest in the animals' welfare.

HOW YOU CAN HELP

Many of the better-known conservation projects tend to be in exotic, far-flung corners of the world. However, conservation work at home is equally important. Anything you can do, no matter how small it may seem at the time, is worth the effort. Here are some ideas:

- Join a local or national conservation organization (particularly one in your area) and take part in some of its activities.

- Set up your own conservation project; for example, if you have a garden, build a bird nestbox or a roosting box for bats and put it up in a suitable place; or create a small nature reserve in one corner, by planting flowers and shrubs which provide food and shelter for birds, butterflies and other animals.

- Feed the birds in your garden with household scraps and other food, particularly during severe winter weather.

- Become a 'wildlife detective' and help your local conservation group to monitor and care for wildlife and habitats which may be threatened in your area.

- Learn more about nature and conservation: watch natural history films, read books and magazines, ask questions.

- Organize a sponsored activity to raise money for a local nature reserve or for an international wildlife conservation project.

- Do not buy coral, stuffed animals, skins, ivory or other products which you know come from threatened animals or threatened habitats. Do not buy exotic pets which you know have been captured in the wild.

- Help with conservation work by caring about the wildlife around you. Do not trample on or pick wild plants, or unnecessarily damage trees. Respect animals, and be kind to them.

BOOKS TO READ

Ayensu, Edward   *Jungles* Jonathan Cape, 1980.

Burton, John A. and Pearson, Bruce   *Rare Mammals of the World* Collins, 1987.

Carwardine, Mark   *The Animal Atlas* Macmillan, 1988.

Curtis, Cecile   *Panda* Frederick Warne, 1976.

Day, David   *The Doomsday Book of Animals* Ebury Press, 1981.

de Havilland, Michael   *The Fabulous Panda* Pan, 1987.

Huxley, Anthony *Green   Inheritance* Collins, 1984.

IUCN   *Red List of Threatened Animals* IUCN Conservation Monitoring Centre, 1988.

King, Peter   *Protect Our Planet* Quiller Press, 1986.

Mountfort, Guy   *Saving the Tiger* Michael Joseph, 1981.

Nichol, John   *The Animal Smugglers* Christopher Helm, 1987.

Penny, Malcolm   *Rhinos: Endangered Species* Christopher Helm, 1987.

Stonehouse, Bernard   *Saving the Animals* Weidenfeld & Nicolson, 1981.

Watson, Lyall   *Sea Guide to Whales of the World* Hutchinson, 1981.

Williams, Heathcote   *Whale Nation* Jonathan Cape, 1988.

WHAT IS A THREATENED SPECIES?

Generally speaking, a *threatened species* is any kind of animal or plant which is so rare that it is in danger of becoming extinct. Many people call these creatures *endangered species*. But conservation organizations have very precise definitions of the different levels of danger to animals and plants, which are summarized here:

Extinct: not definitely seen in the wild during the past 50 years; for example the Tasmanian tiger and the Guam flying fox.

Endangered: in serious or imminent danger of extinction; for example the aye-aye and the mountain gorilla; their survival is unlikely unless immediate action is taken to protect them.

Vulnerable: in danger of extinction and likely to move into the 'endangered' category if nothing is done to protect them; for example the giant anteater and the white-eared pocket mouse.

Rare: not at all common (and therefore at risk) but not yet in serious danger of extinction; for example the giant panda and the Komodo dragon.

Indeterminate: known to be 'endangered', 'vulnerable' or 'rare', but there is not enough information to say which of these three categories is appropriate; for example the marbled cat, the forest owlet and the spider tortoise.

Insufficiently known: suspected but, because of lack of information, not definitely known to belong to any of the above categories; for example the Hercules beetle and the Jamaican flower bat.

(With thanks to the International Union for Conservation of Nature and Natural Resources.)

INDEX